Gramps is Hard of Hearing

Neil and Jane Soslow

Archway Publishing books may be ordered through booksellers or by contacting:

Archway Publishing
1663 Liberty Drive
Bloomington, IN 47403
www.archwaypublishing.com
1 (888) 242-5904

Because of the dynamic nature of the Internet, any web addresses or links contained in this book may have changed since publication and may no longer be valid. The views expressed in this work are solely those of the author and do not necessarily reflect the views of the publisher, and the publisher hereby disclaims any responsibility for them.

Any people depicted in stock imagery provided by Thinkstock are models, and such images are being used for illustrative purposes only. Certain stock imagery © Thinkstock.

ISBN: 978-1-4808-2025-8 (sc)
ISBN: 978-1-4808-2026-5 (hc)
ISBN: 978-1-4808-2027-2 (e)

Print information available on the last page.

Archway Publishing rev. date: 8/11/2015

Dedicated to Amelie, Charlotte and Margaux

"Hi, Gramps! Can we go to the park?" I asked as I ran into my grandfather's house.

"It doesn't look dark to me," said Gramps.

"Dark? No, park."

"Park the car? I think that Grandma parked the car on the side of the house.

We left the driveway open for your Dad's van."

"Not park the car, go to the park." My voice was getting louder.

"Go where?" Gramps asked.

"Park. The Park. The Park down the street!" I shouted. Boy! It was going to be another difficult day with Gramps.

Gramps laughed. "Oh, go to the park! I get it now! Sure." Gramps went to get his hat and his keys. "Let's go."

Gramps and I walked down the street to the park holding hands.

"Guess I was not listening too well when you came in, Caroline. I am hard of hearing and sometimes I only hear some of the sounds people say. Bark, dark, park, quark. Sometimes they all sound the same."

"Those words rhyme, Gramps."

"Yes, and sometimes I just hear the rhyming part and think they are all the same. Must sound pretty weird to someone who hears the whole word."

"I get some words mixed up, too, Gramps. I will try to be more patient when we talk now. You might have to remind me. I get excited."

"And then you talk very fast", said Gramps with a big smile. "I may just have to ask you to slow down a bit, a dit, a fit, a pit." We both giggled. Gramps picked me up and hugged me.

"A bit, Gramps, a bit," I cupped my hand and whispered directly into his ear."

Squeal! Screetch! Eeaaiii!

"What's that?" I asked.

"That was my hearing aid", said Gramps. "Sometimes it squeals when someone gets too close to it or I go to adjust it."

"A hearing aid?"

Gramps reached up and touched one of his ears. "I wear little computers in my ears to help me hear better. Sometimes the sounds just need to be louder. Sometimes they have to be clearer," said Gramps.

"Computers? I have a computer but it won't fit in my ear. Even the computer in my Dad's cell phone wouldn't fit in my ear." We laughed again.

"Here, let me show you my hearing aid," said Gramps. He reached in and took the hearing aid out of his ear. He put it in my hand.

"This is what helps me with those bits and dits and pits and fits. I wear one in each ear. It helps me if you tell me I'm not hearing the right things. Sometimes I can make an adjustment and the words are louder. Sometimes the words can also be clearer."

The hearing aids were very small and I could not imagine how they made Gramps hear better.

"My dad had a hearing problem, too. So did my mom. They both wore hearing aids, too. Guess it comes with getting old."

Gramps adjusted a little button on his hearing aids and put them back into his ears.

"Now can you tell the difference between dark and park? I asked.

"It's a little easier but not perfect. Thank you for being patient."

"Here we are at the dark!" I teased him.

"Park, dear, park", Gramps said as he lifted me up onto the swing.

On the way home, we stopped for ice cream. Gramps liked this ice cream parlor because he said it was very quiet. He could hear me better.

"Thank you for explaining what hard of hearing is, Gramps. I've been thinking. I have a friend in ballet class who is deaf. Is that like being hard of hearing?"

"Yes, it is", said Gramps. "Sometimes people are born without being able to hear. Sometimes it is because of an accident. Sometimes being around loud noises a lot makes someone hard of hearing. I am getting older so my hearing is just wearing out a bit."

FRIEND

LOVE

DANCE

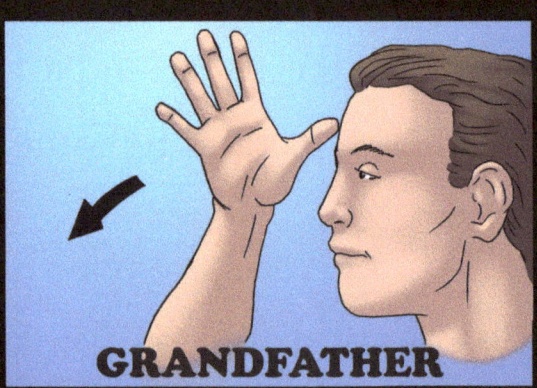

GRANDFATHER

GRANDDAUGHTER

ICE CREAM

Hearing Aid Types

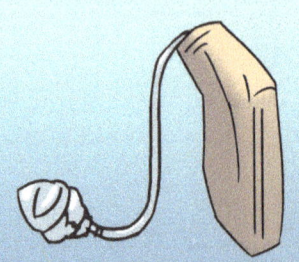  

Behind-The-Ear   Completely-In-Canal   In-The-Canal   In-The-Ear

"She talks with her hands. I know how to do that with her. This means *friend*. This means *love*. This means *dance*."

"This means *grandfather*. This means *granddaughter*. This means *ice cream*," Gramps said.

"Gramps, you know sign language, too?" I was so excited that I could burst.

"Yep. So maybe sometimes if I am really having trouble hearing you, we could just do some signing. I would like to learn some new signs with you."

"Me, too"! I gave Gramps a big hug.

It was a beautiful day with my grandfather.
I'm still smiling. We learn new signs every
time we get together.